Salad

Honor Head

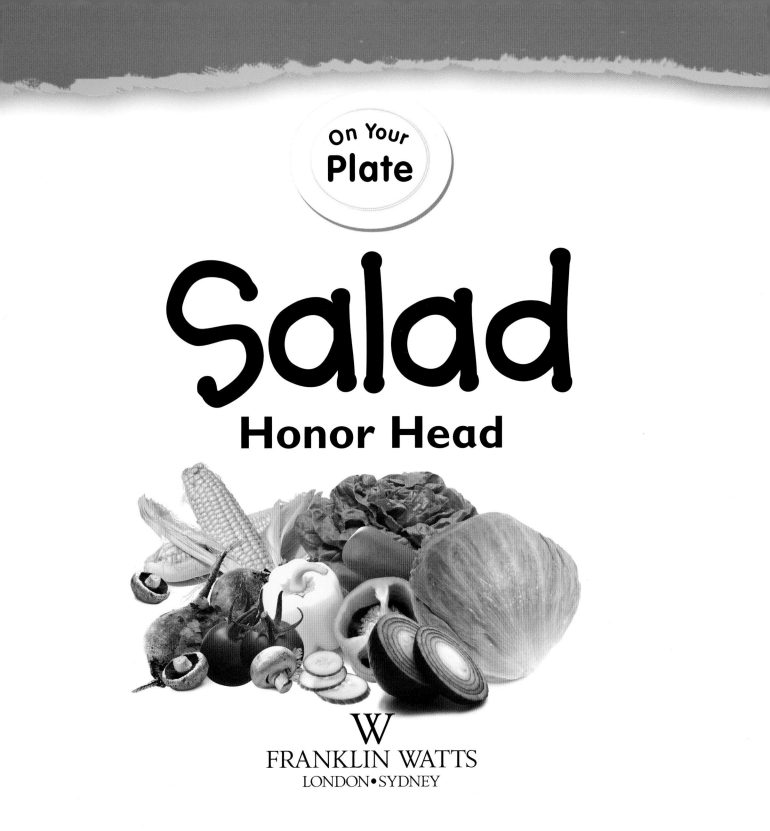

W

FRANKLIN WATTS

LONDON•SYDNEY

First published in 2007 by Franklin Watts

Franklin Watts
338 Euston Road, London NW1 3BH

Franklin Watts Australia
Level 17/207 Kent St, Sydney, NSW 2000

Created by Taglines
Design: Sumit Charles; Harleen Mehta, Q2A Media
Picture research: Pritika Ghura, Q2A Media

ISBN 978 0 7496 7629 2

Dewey classification: 641.8´3

A CIP catalogue for this book is available from the British Library.

Picture credits
t=top b=bottom c=centre l=left r=right m=middle
Cover Images: Shutterstock, Istock and Dreamstime.
Q2A Media: 4b, 17br, Heather Lewis/ Shutterstock: 5t, Anton Gvozdikov/ Shutterstock: 5b, Jacek Chabraszewski/ Shutterstock:
6b, PhantomOfTheOpera/ Istockphoto: 7b, rj lerich/ Shutterstock: 8bl, 15, Og-vision | Dreamstime.com: 8bm, Marc Dietrich/
Shutterstock: 8br, Juriah Mosin/ Shutterstock: 9, Joe Gough/ Istockphoto: 11bl, Alex Balako/ Shutterstock: 11br, Isatori |
Dreamstime.com: 12, Antonio Jorge Nunes/ Shutterstock: 13, Joss | Dreamstime.com: 14, khwi/ Shutterstock: 16, Andriy Doriy/
Shutterstock: 17bl, Danny Smythe/ Shutterstock: 18, Clay Clifford/ Shutterstock: 19, Leon Forado/ Shutterstock: 20, Paul
Schneider/ Shutterstock: 21, Roman Sigaev/ Shutterstock: 22.

Printed in China

Franklin Watts is a division of Hachette Children's Books,
an Hachette Livre UK company.

Contents

What is salad?

A salad is a mix of vegetables or fruit. We usually eat salads cold.

  Salads are tasty on their own or with a main meal.

Cherry tomatoes can be eaten whole in a salad.

You can put juicy tomatoes in a salad. These are very good for you.

Cucumbers

Cucumbers have a rough, green skin. You can eat the skin.

seeds

There are tiny seeds inside a cucumber.

Gherkins can be chopped into a salad for extra flavour.

Gherkins are young cucumbers. They are pickled in vinegar.

Green salad

A green salad is a mix of lettuce and other green leaves.

iceberg lettuce

cos lettuce

round lettuce

There are lots of different types of lettuce.

You can eat green salad as a snack or as a side dish with your main meal.

Add cherry tomatoes and cucumber to a green salad for a filling lunch.

Onions

Spring onions are onions that are picked before they are fully grown.

Try some spring onion chopped in your salad.

Red onions look pretty. They do not taste as strong as other onions.

 Red onion rings are used to decorate salads.

11

Beetroot

Beetroot is cooked before it is eaten cold.

Beetroot grows in the ground.

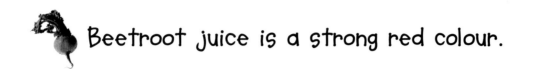 Beetroot juice is a strong red colour.

beetroot

Eating beetroot helps you to get well quickly after a cold or illness.

Peppers

You can buy green, red, orange and yellow peppers.

The white bits inside a pepper are thrown away.

Try eating peppers cut into strips with some tasty dips.

 Slices of pepper make a crunchy lunchbox treat.

Sweetcorn

When sweetcorn is picked it is covered by a husk. Inside are the sweetcorn kernels.

kernel

husk

Sweetcorn like this is called corn on the cob.

Sweetcorn kernels are sold in tins. You can sprinkle them on to salads.

Sweetcorn kernels are sometimes called niblets.

Mushrooms

Mushrooms grow in damp places. Fresh mushrooms are eaten raw in salads.

 Big mushrooms have a strong flavour.

18

Before you eat mushrooms, always wash or wipe away any bits of earth.

 Sliced mushrooms are good to eat in salads or in sandwiches.

Celery

Long sticks of celery grow in bunches above the ground.

Most people eat the pale celery stalks. They do not eat the green leaves.

Munching on celery can help your teeth and gums to stay strong.

Try peanut butter with crunchy sticks of celery.

Things to do

Salad bowl puzzle

Can you recognise what is in this salad bowl?

Oh no!

All of this salad has been covered in beetroot juice. What colour should the vegetables be?

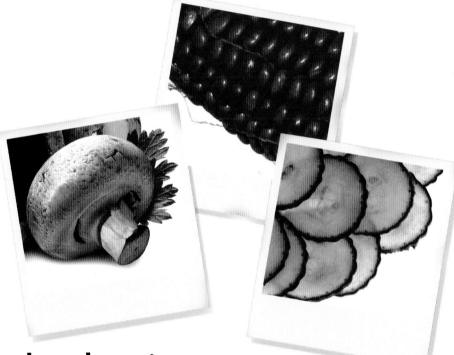

Salad selection

Can you guess what is in this salad from these descriptions?

a)   I am long and green with small seeds inside.

b)   I am red and juicy.

c)   I am crunchy and have green leaves.

23

Glossary

husk
The covering on the outside of the corn which you do not eat.

pickled
A food that is put into vinegar to make it last a long time.

seeds
New plants grow from the seeds inside a fruit or vegetable.

Index